RJG Productions present

C000194266

A Hundred Words for Snow

by Tatty Hennessy

A Hundred Words for Snow was first performed at the Arcola Theatre, London, on 9 January 2018, as part of Heretic Voices. A new production was performed at VAULT Festival 2018.

In February 2019, *A Hundred Words for Snow* toured to Warwick Arts Centre, The Mill Studio at Guildford's Yvonne Arnaud, Aldeburgh Jubilee Hall, The Spring Havant, The Garage Norwich and Riverfront Newport, ending in a full run at Trafalgar Studios 2 in London's West End.

A Hundred Words for Snow

by Tatty Hennessy

CAST

RORY   Gemma Barnett

COMPANY

Director   Lucy Jane Atkinson
Designer   Christianna Mason
Lighting Designer   Lucy Adams
Sound Designer   Mark Sutcliffe
Associate Sound Designer   Annie May Fletcher
Producer (RJG Productions)   Rebecca Gwyther
Stage Manager   Bryony Byrne

Graphic Designer   Madison Clare
Production Photographer   Nick Rutter

Supported by

Peggy Ramsay Foundation and Arts Council England

With thanks to

VAULT Festival, Felicity Aston, Rose Wardlaw, all of our parents,
Mobius PR, JHI Marketing, Eline Hallem, Charlotte Vaight,
Elke Mienert, Hilde and Bomsa, and the benevolent ghosts of
Wanny Woldstad and Fridtjof Nansen.

BIOGRAPHIES

GEMMA BARNETT | RORY

Training: Oxford School of Drama, First Class Hons Drama, University of East Anglia.

Stage credits: Lola in *Lola*, Rory in *A Hundred Words for Snow* (VAULT Festival); Cinderella in *Cinderella: A Wicked Mother of a Night Out* (Not Too Tame Theatre); Beatrice in *Foxing* (Pint Sized); 1 in *Flog* (Camden People's Theatre); Charlie in *Roosting* (Park Theatre); Kelly in *Oil and Matter* (The Bunker); Billie in *Cousins* (Soho Theatre); Heavenly in *Spring Storm* (The North Wall).

Film credits: Elsa in *Versions of Us* (short film, Lizzy Mansfield); Jess in *Night Shift* (short film, Dylan Brown).

Other credits: Billie in *The Noble Nine* (rehearsed reading, NW Productions, Kelly in *Oil and Matter* (rehearsed reading, The Bunker).

Credits whilst training: Olivia in *Twelfth Night*, Carla in *The Wasp*, Miss Cooper in *Separate Tables*.

TATTY HENNESSY | WRITER

Tatty Hennessy is an award-winning playwright and dramaturg. She is a graduate of the Royal Court Young Writers' Programme. Previous work includes *All That Lives* (Ovalhouse); *The Snow Queen* (Theatre N16) and *F Off* (National Youth Theatre). This is her first published play.

LUCY JANE ATKINSON | DIRECTOR

Lucy Jane Atkinson is an award-winning theatre director, focused primarily on new writing. She has directed work by acclaimed playwrights Camilla Whitehill, John O'Donovan, Tristan Bernays, Isley Lynn and Barry McStay, among others.

Her recent work includes directing *A Hundred Words for Snow* by Tatty Hennessy, *Testament* by Tristan Bernays, and *Vespertilio* by Barry McStay, all at VAULT Festival in London. Her work at the festival over the past two years led to her being named number one on *The Stage*'s list of talents to watch from VAULT 2018, stating '*her direction is acutely sensitive to the shifting energy of the writing. Evident but never overbearing.*'

CHRISTIANNA MASON | DESIGNER

Christianna Mason is a theatre designer and artist based in London. Originally from Northern Ireland she has an international background having grown up in Belgium. She trained at the Royal Academy of Dramatic Art, following a BA Hons in Drama and Theatre Studies, and a Foundation in Fine Art. Since graduating Christianna has worked in theatre, opera, drama schools, youth work, and installation art. She often draws on sculpture, art history and unusual textures for inspiration. Recent set and costume design credits include: *Romeo and Juliet* (Dynamo Theatre, Zürich); *To Father a Nation* (Rich Mix); *Blood Wedding* (Omnibus Theatre); *Boatswain's Mate* (Arcola Theatre) and *Always Right There* (George Bernard Shaw Theatre).

MARK SUTCLIFFE | SOUND DESIGNER

Mark graduated from LAMDA's Technical Theatre & Stage Management FdA course, where his sound designs included: *A Few Good Men*, *King John*, *Othello*, *Macbeth*, *Measure for Measure* and *Sweeney Todd*.

His recent work includes: sound design on *Mary's Babies* (VAULT Festival/ Old Red Lion Theatre); *CAUSE, Testament* (VAULT Festival); *On Set with Viacom* (Ambika P3); *Where Do Little Birds Go?* (Old Red Lion Theatre); *The Machine* (Tristan Bates Theatre) and *Resilience* (UK tour).

Production Sound Engineer on: *Matilda the Musical* (UK & Ireland tour); *The Girl from the North Country* (Noël Coward Theatre); *The Exorcist* (Phoenix Theatre); *Who's Afraid of Virginia Woolf?* (Harold Pinter Theatre) and *Alice's Adventures Underground* (The Vaults).

ANNIE MAY FLETCHER | ASSOCIATE SOUND DESIGNER

Annie graduated from LAMDA's Technical Theatre & Stage Management FdA course. She is the Laboratory Associate Sound Designer at Nuffield Southampton Theatre 2018/19 and an Associate Artist with Snapper Theatre company.

LUCY ADAMS | LIGHTING DESIGNER

Lucy Adams is a London-based lighting designer. She regularly collaborates with ThisEgg, having designed *Goggles*, *Me and My Bee*, *UNCONDITIONAL* and *dressed.* for the company. She's also worked with BREACH Theatre on *It's True, It's True, It's True*; Barrel Organ on *Anyone's Guess How We Got Here*; YESYESNONO on *[insert slogan here]* and Haley McGee on *Ex-Boyfriend Yard Sale*. Her lighting design for new writing includes: *Tumulus* by Christopher Adams, directed by Matt Steinberg; *Skin A Cat* by Isley Lynn directed by Blythe Stewart, and *One Jewish Boy* by Stephen Laughton, directed by Sarah Meadows.

REBECCA GWYTHER | PRODUCER

Rebecca is a freelance theatre producer. She runs RJG Productions and is co-director of Old Sole Theatre Company.

Current work includes: *A Hundred Words for Snow* (Trafalgar Studios/UK tour/ VAULT Festival); *Anna X* (VAULT Festival) and Research & Development of *Scum* (Park Theatre).

Previous work includes: *Misfire* (Cardiff Fringe & Ventnor Fringe); *Precisionism* (Sligo, Ireland/The Hope Theatre); *What Goes on in Front of Closed Doors* (Pleasance Courtyard/UK tour); *Finders Keepers* for Hot Coals Theatre Ensemble (ZOO); *Headways Festival* (The Albany, Deptford) and *Glockenspiel* (Tristan Bates Theatre).

BRYONY BYRNE | STAGE MANAGER
Bryony Byrne is a freelance stage manager working in the UK and abroad.
She's worked with the award-winning Wardrobe Ensemble (*Education,
Education, Education*) and on the world's longest-running live comedy show,
NewsRevue. Other work includes *Rachel* (Trestle Theatre); *Derailed* (Little
Soldier Productions) and *Our Country* by the experimental LA-based company
Wilderness. She also works with individual artists such as comedian Alison
Thea-Skot (*BBC Culture Show*) and Hugh McCann (resident artist at *Kaleider*).
Prior to her stage-management work, she produced and wrote a feature
comedy film, *Akela*, which was awarded Best Screenplay at the Vancouver
Golden Panda Film Festival. She also performs regularly with improv group,
Night Bus, at the Free Association in London.

A HUNDRED WORDS FOR SNOW

Tatty Hennessy

Farthest North

I've always been a bit obsessed with Polar Exploration, people pushing themselves to extremes, risking and often losing their lives in the pursuit of knowledge. It seems all the more poignant now, as we continue to come to terms with our hand in climate change and disaster – this landscape used to lay waste to us, and now we destroy it. Which may, in turn, destroy us. I wanted to write a story that probed at this. What does it mean to be an explorer of the world? How do we relate to the planet and each other? What world will we leave for the generations after us? How do we come to terms with what we've already lost? And I knew I wanted a hero at the centre of that story who wasn't like the explorers we're used to seeing in the history books. The wild, baffling, lonely, improbable landscape of the Arctic felt like quite a natural place to explore the similar landscape of girlhood and adolescence, and of grief. Rory was born.

While writing *A Hundred Words for Snow* I was lucky enough to receive a grant from the Peggy Ramsay Foundation to travel to Tromsø and Svalbard to follow in Rory's footsteps. It was a strange and exhilarating trip. By way of an introduction to these two pieces, which I think represent two extremes of despair and ultimately hope on the subject of the Arctic, Nick Hern Books have kindly allowed me to print some extracts from the diary I kept of the trip, and how the north itself shaped these plays.

Tatty Hennessy
January 2019

10 August 2017

I am currently eating a sandwich in a little park in the centre of Tromsø, in Norway, beneath a seagull be-shitten statue of polar explorer Roald Amundsen. It's hard to describe how it feels to follow the path of a character I invented. Like I imagined my way here. Stopped for a coffee earlier and saw a woman who looks *exactly* like Frida. Or rather Frida will now look exactly like her.

Yesterday I took myself to the Tromsø Polar Museum (like Rory!). Lots of mannequins of seal-trappers swinging axes at stuffed baby seals. Black-and-white photos of a fox being peeled. A vacant-looking mannequin woman in a fur stole just captioned 'The consumer'. A polar-bear heart in a jar.

There's a grave. A replica of a grave site of a British or Dutch whaler, discovered on Svalbard and preserved by the ice. His mouth is wide open and his teeth are all intact but there's just a bundle of bones where his feet used to be. Behind him is a corny painted pantomime backdrop of mountains and midnight-sun sky. Next to him is a pile of whale bones. His prey. I tried to imagine the moment whoever buried him had to turn around and go.

There's a whole room on Nansen, and lots of photographs of Wanny Woldstad (mounted on a pink wall...) and inspirational lines like 'She made the trappers' homes nicer by bringing tablecloths and cooking for them', proving that the unequal division of emotional labour is rife in all climates, and even being able to kill and skin a polar bear single-handed is no defence. There's also a model of a ship called the *MS Polarfart* which is funny whoever you are. Took a trip to Polaria; a tired aquarium whose star attraction is some rather sad-looking seals torpedoing apathetically over a green-grimed underwater walkway. The *MS Polstjerna* is more interesting; a perfectly preserved 1940s seal-hunting ship in a fake-ice landscape. Amazing how the history of white people in the Arctic is so inextricably bound in violence against it. There's an accompanying exhibition about the techniques Nansen and Amundsen learned from the Inuit, how to adapt their sledges, to hunt, what clothes to wear. Apparently 'anorak' comes from the

Inuit word 'anore' (wind) and 'anguloq' (birdskin), and 'kayak' comes from the Inuit word 'qajaq' which means 'man's boat', even though they were usually made by women.

At night (such as night is, more of an unending sunset) I went up Fløya, the mountain across the river. Every step further up the beauty doubles. The clouds looked so much like snow it felt like if I lay on my back I could walk on them.

I'm understanding Rory more.

13 August

Just landed in Svalbard. I haven't stopped shaking since we landed. It is terrifying here. Like the mountains are just waiting to fall on us. This is the end of the human world. What can a human life mean here?

It seems utterly meaningless here that we can take any power from the things we leave behind, from what lasts. The only power we have is in what passes.

It's illegal to die in Svalbard because you can't be buried – bodies don't rot in the permafrost. The ground doesn't even want our corpses.

Polar bears still attack people here. It's illegal to kill them and illegal to die so I imagine as well as being fucking terrifying being attacked by a polar bear would also present a bewildering legal dilemma.

I could never have imagined it would feel like this. What am I doing.

15 August

Yesterday I walked on Foxfonna glacier with a guide (Hilde) and an out-of-season sled dog (Bomsa). Bomsa means teddy bear. I feel like bears are everywhere.

We hiked up the mountain over rocks like the surface of Mars, like walking on a scaly alien's back, covered in orange-black-green lichen and white crumbly reindeer moss. Even here, things grow. We passed a big observation station with impossible-looking vast satellite dishes. The mouth of the fjord below and the mountains were the only thing in all directions. None of this feels people-sized. Then we saw the glacier itself loom ahead, a threshold. We stepped over the line onto the ice like through a portal to another world, just empty white. Stopping for the strangest lunch of my life, hunkered down with packets of pasta and hot Ribena, washing our spoons by dipping them into the ice, looking out at nothing but white in all directions. My boots are not as waterproof as I might have hoped. I would have been a shit explorer.

17 August

The sun hasn't set at all while I've been here. Last night I went to a bar in town and drank a cognac (they sell a Nansen cognac, I'm only human) with two engineers, on their way out to Ny-Ålesund, the northernmost permanently inhabited point in the world. Even the name seems desolate to me. Leaving in the middle of the night to bright sun is wonderfully baffling. It's like the slate never gets cleaned, never reset, everything is always as it is with no concern at all for our little rhythms.

Even Longyearbyen itself feels temporary, like a goldrush town which I suppose it is but with coal in place of gold. Set into a valley beneath spidery old mining stations jutting out of the mountains. There's a little graveyard on the edge of town. Neat rows of little white crosses, from before the law was passed. Miners, probably. Bleak place to be left.

18 August

Took a trip to Pyramiden, an abandoned Russian mining town, on the brilliantly named *MS Polargirl*. Three hours there, up on deck, cold cold cold. I mean obviously it's cold, but it is *cold*. Got talking to another man travelling alone and turns out he's a geography teacher. Although he wasn't all that enthused when I exclaimed: 'That's amazing! The dead dad in my play is a geography teacher!' You live and learn. He's taking a course at the university in Longyearbyen on climate change. He talked to me about albedo, glaciation and tectonic drift, how this is the best place in the world to do field work. I like to think that in the future Rory is like this.

We arrived at Pyramiden in persistent grey, icy drizzle to be met by a Russian guard with a rifle beneath a colour-leeched Soviet-era statue: 'Welcome, friends, to lovely Russia.' As well as a functional mining outpost this was a propaganda town. Beautiful wood-clad buildings, a hospital, free food to workers. They even flew in soil so the grass would literally be greener on the Russian side of the fjord. We got to look around the old culture house; a grand ruin, abandoned seemingly mid-moment, with posters and plates and magazines still strewn around, and deflated footballs in the gymnasium. There's even a theatre. A self-consciously grand thoroughfare runs through the centre of the town overlooked by a stern statue of Lenin: 'The locals call it the Champs-Élysées,' says our guide. Ten people live here all year round. Three in winter. It used to be hundreds. They used to have the world's northernmost swimming pool. Now they have the world's northernmost dry swimming pool.

After pulling out of town we sailed past the edge of a glacier. The sun came out and made the ice shine blue. Forty feet high at the thinnest point, muddy and cragged and electric. Burning cold. Geography teacher and I thought we saw an actual, real-life polar bear on the shore, but even through his binoculars it was only a small white smudge. Could have been a trick of the light. We'll never know.

Note on the Text

Rory talks directly to us.

The only necessary props are 'Dad' (an urn of ashes) and a copy of Fridtjof Nansen's *Farthest North*. When Rory speaks to Dad, she addresses the urn.

Where another character speaks, this is Rory playing both parts.

RORY, *female, fifteen*.

When you get to the end of something, it's hard to remember the
start. Hard to remember how it began. Like, what was the first
step? And how far back do you go? I got on a plane. And before
that, a train, and before that, I walked. I took the ashes after
I found the journal after I went into Dad's study after the
crematorium curtains shut which was all after I sat at the kitchen
table and stared at a spoon when Mum said that he'd died. Which
was after he died. But even that's not the start, is it? How can that
be the start? Because the notebook wouldn't have existed without
the history and the history wouldn't have happened without the
geography and none of it would've happened at all if all the skin
of the world hadn't cooled and settled the way that it did and the
oceans hadn't flowed the way that they do and the ice didn't
freeze the way that it does, if the earth hadn't stopped exactly this
far from the sun, if the sun never formed then I, Rory, me, here,
hello, would never have been sitting watching my mum cry in a
helicopter in a snowstorm with my dad's ashes at the North Pole.

Jesus you already look lost. Okay. Here goes. Strap in.

My name is Rory.

Yes, I know that's a boy's name.

Yes that is my real name.

Yes, really.

Oh, alright. Full name. If you really need to know; Aurora. Yes.
Aurora.

Mortifying.

I swear the only people who like weird names are people with
names like Bob or Sue or Tim. You like it? Try living with it.
It's weird to think Mum wanted me to be the kind of person
who'd suit the name 'Aurora'. I wouldn't want to meet that
person, would you? Sounds like a right bint.

I've totally forgiven her, as you can tell. Joking.

Nobody calls me Aurora. Call me Rory and we'll get on fine.

And this – (*The urn.*)

Is Dad.

Say hello, Dad.

Dad doesn't say anything.

He's shy.

RORY *gives us a small smile. She's testing us.*

Used to be a lot more talkative. Didn't you, Dad? Lost a bit of weight, too.

Balances the urn on her outstretched hand.

It's weird a whole person's in there.

This is Dad's story, really.

He died. Obviously. Car accident. Walking home from school. He's a teacher. At my school. I know. Mortifying. And a geography teacher. The worst. Sorry, Dad, but it's true. They didn't let me see the body before we got him cremated. ~~I say 'we' but I didn't have anything to do with it, and actually if you ask me I think he'd've hated being inside a shitty urn for eternity but nobody did ask me did they so here he is.~~ The funeral was fucking awful. The coffin like, slides behind these red curtains, and all I could think about was how many other people must've been burned in there and how unless they're really good at sweeping there's probably little bits of other people still in there with him and I wondered who they were and what their family thought about when the curtain shut. Mum did a reading but she was a total state, like, crying so much she couldn't even get the words out which was actually a blessing cos the poem she'd chosen was rubbish. He would've hated it. And all my dad's work friends which basically meant all my teachers coming to ours for sandwiches and relatives I never see saying empty things like 'oh well, wasn't it a lovely service' and I'm like actually my mum cried so much she couldn't string a sentence together and then they burned my dad in a fire so lovely isn't really the word for it, Aunt Carol.

I didn't say that. Obviously. I made the tea. People can't talk to you if you're busy making tea. And if they try you just say 'Sugar?' like that and they get distracted. I went to stand in the garden, just, breathe a bit and fucking Mum's out there. Crying. Again. Leaving me to talk to everyone by myself. Very responsible. I go to leave as soon as I see her but she's already seen me so I'm stuck and –

MUM. Hello, darling.

She says. Since when does she call me 'darling'.

RORY. Alright.

Pause.

MUM. D'you want a cup of tea?

RORY. No thank you.

Pause.

RORY. Great.

When there was a lull in conversation Dad used to hold his hands up like this –

RORY *waves her hands like claws and makes a little bear sound.*

Awkward paws.

I don't say that.

MUM. It's nice how many people came.

She says.

RORY. Yeah.

I say.

RORY. What are we gonna do with Dad?

We brought him back from the crematorium and he was just like, on the kitchen table.

Mum sort of flinches.

RORY. He can't stay in the kitchen, can he?

MUM. Rory. Just. Not now. Please.

RORY. Like a bloody pepper mill.

MUM. Rory. (*Beat*.) I'll figure something out.

She says.

MUM. Just. Leave it. For now.

Her face is red from crying. She's looking at me, with this funny look, like she's trying to remember my face. And then she looks away and she says.

MUM. It was a lovely service, wasn't it.

And I go all cold inside. And I say.

RORY. No. It was rubbish.

And I go inside and up to my room and I don't come down again till morning.

And when I come back down the kitchen is quiet. All the guests have left. Mum's in her room. Hiding from me. I feel bad, like I should apologise, make us breakfast or something but then.

Dad's on the kitchen table. In his urn. Just. Left there. So I'm gonna have to deal with him, am I?

I pick him up. I can hold him in one hand. He feels cold.

You can't stay in here, Dad. People eat in here. Nothing personal but it's creepy. Come on.

I decide to take him to his study. You can wait there, Dad, till we figure out what to do with you. I pause at the door. I half-imagine I'm gonna open it and he'll be sitting there in his dressing gown, leant over marking some workbooks. But that's stupid cos he's in my hand, isn't he?

I open the door. And it's his study. And nothing's changed.

The thing about my dad is, he was an explorer. Not literally of course. Literally he was a geography teacher but in his mind. And not these shitty TV explorers who drink piss for the cameras, like Bear Grylls, god what a bell-end, no, like a proper old-school explorer. Mungo Park or Shackleton, you know? The-blank-bits-on-the-map explorer. That's who he really was, inside. When I was little we'd go to the woods and pretend we were the first people ever to go there. Take our compasses and cheese

sandwiches and make our own maps, mark trees with chalk. He'd
set me treasure hunts, put an X on the map and I'd have to get us
there, and we'd arrive and the treasure would be, like, an
interesting tree he liked or a river with some notable erosion. I'd
try to get him to give me clues, tell me what it was we were
looking for, but he'd just say, 'We'll know it when we get there.'
He taught me to figure out north from the stars. The Pole Star. If
you know where north is, you can always find home, he said.

His favourite was the North. The North Pole. Explorers like
Franklin and Peary hauling sleds over ice. Polar bears and furs
and scurvy and Inuit. Have to call them Inuit, not Eskimos,
according to Dad. And when I was little I thought it was ace.
We'd build igloos in the garden and he'd pretend to be a polar
bear and chase me, and I tried to imagine it, a place where
men's tongues froze to their beards, where houses were made
out of blocks of ice, the ground under your feet could crack
open and swallow you whole. You know how all kids avoid
cracks in the pavement? Mine were cracks in the ice.

But I got a bit old for it all, you know. And anyway it was only
pretend exploring. I've got all the maps of everything on my
phone, now. It's all finished. No blank places left. Exploring
now is drinking piss for the cameras. He was born in the wrong
time, my dad. That's what someone should have said about him,
at the funeral.

We stopped going on our adventures. I took down the maps
from my walls. And I'd sort of forgotten about it. The North and
the snow and the beards. But I carry Dad into his study and
there it all is. Maps of the Arctic Circle and posters of beardy
men in thick furs looking moody, articles and clippings about
global warming all over the walls, books and books and more
books with big bold font on the spines. Man's books. Dad's
books. And there on the desk is his notebook.

His journal.

His pen is on the desk next to it. It's okay to read someone's
diary if they're dead, right? Like, we read Anne Frank's in
school. So.

I put Dad down on the desk. I sit in his chair. I look at the
notebook. I open it.

'North Pole Trip.'

It says.

North Pole Trip.

And I remember.

I remember lying in our makeshift igloo on white sheets for snow. I remember Dad saying, 'One day. One day we'll go, Rory. When you're older. Would you like that?' I don't remember saying yes.

I flick through the notebook. Careful plans. Weather charts. Tour operators, chartered-flight companies. Names of strange places. Barneo. Longyearbyen. Cost estimates. For two travellers.

(*To Dad*.) You planned it.

'North Pole Trip.' It says. And 'Next year.'

Next to the notebook, a book with a black-and-white cover, a photograph of a young man with serious facial hair and deep eyes staring out at me. *Farthest North* by Fridtjof Nansen. I remember this book. Dad used to read it to me instead of a bedtime story. A great Polar explorer, one of Dad's faves. Some of the pages are dog-eared, folded down. I open to one. He's underlined passages in blue and black ink.

'Alas! Alas! Life is full of disappointments; as one reaches one ridge there is always another and a higher one beyond which blocks the view.'

Well fuck that.

Fuck that. Fuck disappointment. Suddenly it's all so clear. What to do with him.

(*To Dad*.) Dad. You never got to go. But I can take you.

So it's not *quite* as tricky to get to the North Pole now, but it's still bloody hard. I've got to look at the maps, make a plan. It'll be like an old treasure hunt, right, Dad? And I figure if I'm going to go, I can learn a bit from the people who went before. The beardy men. And it's funny, a lot feels familiar, half-remembered. The names come back to be quickly. The facts and stories Dad told me coming back in dribs and drabs. Like that thing about Inuit having thousands of words for snow? You probably heard that one. Well it's total bullshit. A myth. Anthropologists making shit up. Funny what mistakes get stuck like that.

And a lot of is totally new, and totally insane. Like did you know there's not just one North Pole? Oh no. There's *five*. Five North Poles. And they're all in different places. I know. So the first thing I have to do is Pick a Pole.

Pole number one: Geographic North Pole, that's the one at the top of the globe or 'where the earth's axis of rotation meets its surface' thank you, Wikipedia. The northernmost point on earth. Ninety degrees north. In the middle of a constantly freezing, shifting and thawing fourteen-thousand-feet-deep ocean, seven hundred kilometres away from the nearest land, eight hundred and seventeen kilometres away from the nearest inhabited land. Difficult.

Pole number two: Magnetic North Pole. That's where all the compasses point to, and it's never actually in the same place twice because the magnetic field is always changing. So I might get all the way there find out it's actually moved to Greenland or something. Really difficult.

Pole number three: The Geomagnetic North Pole. The centre of the earth's magnetic field. Wikipedia says it's where the 'lines of attraction enter the earth' which sounds like geography innuendo and is therefore gross. Also I'm not completely sure I understand what it actually is, so going there is difficult.

Pole number four: The Pole of Inaccessibility. Not a promising title. The remotest place from any other place. Supremely difficult.

And Pole number five: The Celestial Pole. An imaginary point in the sky where the earth's point of rotation, extended upwards, meets the celestial sphere. Directly above your head if you stand at the Pole. Sounds like it'd be the most beautiful. But probably not realistic unless I grow wings. Impossible.

So. Geographical North it has to be.

One explorer thought the North Pole was a hole leading down into an underground world actually inhabited by other living things.

It sounds nuts but nobody really knew what was up there. Volcanoes, islands, spikes, warm oceans, people thought *everything* might be there except the one thing that actually is there. Which is nothing.

Because there's nothing there. It's just ice.

Here is a photo in case you don't believe me.

See. Nothing.

My gran once went on a cruise across the Atlantic and when they got to the place where the *Titanic* sank the captain made an announcement and everyone rushed to the railings to take a photograph of the bit of ocean where the *Titanic* sank. Gran showed me the photo and it's just water. Obviously. Nothing to tell you it's special. Same with the Pole. There's nothing actually there.

And people *died* finding that nothing. Like, a lot of people.

William Barents, stranded for a year on Nova Zembla, died.

Vitus Bering. Leader of the Great Northern Expedition. Stranded on an island off Russia. Died.

John Franklin. British naval officer and expedition commander of the quite frankly asking-for-it *HMS Terror*. Lost for years on the ice off King William Island. Died.

And that's just for starters. That's not even counting all the people who died looking for the people who had died. And that's just the captains, the crew died too. Most of the bodies were never found either so the whole ice pack's a bit like a big fridge-freezer full of dead explorers, and maybe when the ice melts their bones fall out and sink.

Because there are a *lot* of ways to die in the Arctic. And most of them are slow. For starters, it's fucking cold. Obviously. One guy, Peter Freuchen, spent a whole Arctic winter in a little hut all by himself. And it was so cold that his breath froze to the walls. And when they came back to find him he was almost completely trapped, because the walls were so thick with his frozen breath. And they had to break him out with chisels.

And another time he was out walking in a snowstorm and he dug a hole to escape the blizzard and pulled his coat on top of it but the hole froze shut and he couldn't get out so he did a shit and moulded the shit into a chisel shape and waited for it to freeze and then hacked his way out of the ice with his own shit-chisel.

So yeah. It's cold. And frostbite is nasty. Your blood vessels and nerves freeze. And then there's scurvy, which is literally no picnic.

On Elisha Kane's trip, twenty of the men died of rabies they caught off a sled-dog.

Franklin's men ate each other.

People still get killed by polar bears.

Nansen called it 'Helheim'– (*Reading from Nansen.*) 'a place where the death-goddess holds her sway, the abyss at the world's end, the shore of corpses where no living creature can draw breath.'

Looks at Dad.

That's where you wanna go?

Why?

I guess I'll know when I get there.

I reckon I'll go via Norway – that's where Nansen's from. I can almost follow his exact journey. First I'll fly to Tromsø, way up in the North, and then get a flight to Longyearbyen, the capital of the island of Svalbard. I know. Epic. From there I have to get on a charter flight to Barneo, the Russian base at the eighty-ninth degree. That's the last place you can fly to before you ski or sledge the last sixty kilometres to the Pole.

Easy.

(*To Dad.*) We'll figure it out.

(*Still to Dad, sheepishly.*) I'm taking Mum's credit card. I know, but. I can't ask her, can I? And she didn't ask me before putting you in there so I don't have to ask her. She got her shitty funeral now I'm gonna do it right.

I try to learn a bit of Norwegian, just in case. Turns out the word for 'bear' is *bjorn* which basically means that guy in ABBA was called Bear. (*To Dad.*) D'you think we'll see a bear? We're going at the right time apparently. Springtime. In the winter there's literally no sun at all, it goes beneath the horizon and just stays there. I don't even like it when I come out of school and it's dark outside so that sounds like a nightmare. And then in summertime the ice isn't so easy to cross cos it gets a bit slushy and you sink into it. Springtime is Goldilocks – just right. Bears coming out of their winter dens. Plus I figure a lone teenager in an airport is less fishy in the Easter holidays.

Night before leaving, I go up to the attic, dig out my big coat, compass and my old backpack from our treasure hunting days. I pack up everything I think I'll need, make a checklist like Dad would've done, and check it all off the night before.

Passport. Check.
Money. Check.
Torch. Check.
Batteries. Check.
Vitamin-C pills. Check.
Maps. Check.
Jumpers. Check.
Socks. Check.
Nansen. Check.
Dad. Check.

I think that's everything.

I hear Mum come up the stairs and I push the backpack under my bed. She pushes the door open and looks in at me.

MUM. You alright?

She asks.

RORY. Yeah.

MUM. Need anything.

RORY. No thanks.

MUM. Do you want to go back to school after the holidays? Must be lonely here.

RORY. I'm alright.

MUM. Well. Let me know.

RORY. Yeah

MUM. Goodnight.

RORY. Night.

She gives me this look, like she's about to say something else but thinks better of it and shuts the door.

Maybe RORY *does the 'awkward paws' action here.*

She's just gonna think I've run away. (*To Dad.*) Once we've gone, there's no coming back till we've done it, Dad. No second chances.

Next morning I wait till I hear her shut the front door. I make myself wait fifteen minutes in case she comes back. She doesn't. Am I really doing it? Are we really gonna do it, Dad?

Dad would look to the beardy dead men for inspo.

(*Reading from Nansen.*) 'The difficult is what takes a little time. The impossible is what takes a little longer.'

Sounds good to me.

I step off the bus in Tromsø and it's just kind of normal. There are like house and cafés and office-supply shops and everything. I was expecting something a bit, I dunno, *arctic* and wild. Hardly feels intrepid exploring somewhere with a tourist information centre.

But you wanted to come here, Dad. This was the last place Nansen stopped before he set off for the ice. Let's be tourists for a bit. Just you and me. I feel kind of giddy. It's nice being alone in a strange place. I have this lightness in my chest like a helium heart. I go and sit on a bench by the river. Can you see,

Dad? On the horizon in all directions there's green mountains topped with snow, and little houses across the water. The light is funny, different to light in London, it's sort of, I dunno, clean light, although I never thought of London light as cloudy before but it must've been cos suddenly it's like the world is in HD.

I decide to take Dad to the Tromsø Polar Museum. You'll like that. There's a big German school group arriving just as I do so I sort of manage to slink in amongst them without paying. They've got a whole room on Nansen, Dad! Pages from his actual journal! His handwriting's bad as yours. There he is, standing with his foot up on an ice floe, staring back at his ship stuck in the ice, miles of empty white around him.

OLD MAN. Hello there!

I jump out of my skin. There's an old man behind me, smiling.

OLD MAN. Do you speak English?

I consider for a moment attempting a German accent but quickly decide against it and just nod.

OLD MAN. I think your schoolmates are upstairs already.

RORY. Okay.

I mumble.

OLD MAN. Here, let me show you something.

He takes me over to a corner of the room full of old photos of a woman in snow gear looking at the camera with her eyes closed. Must've been rubbish before you could delete bad photos.

OLD MAN. 'That's Wanny Woldstad. The first woman trapper to overwinter in Svalbard. Women were explorers too!'

He looks at me like I have some inspirational disability and gestures at the photos. A woman in snow furs, holding a rifle, killing a bear. All mounted on a pink display board.

RORY. Cool.

I say. But it's hardly the same as Nansen. The sign says as well as being the first trapper she was Tromsø's first female taxi driver which is just tragic. Like when Mrs Harris put a big poster of Ada Lovelace on the wall and obviously someone drew a dick near her mouth the same lunchtime and she had to take it down. (*To Dad*.) Did you know about Wanny Woldstad?

We've caught up with the school group now and the teacher's giving a lecture. The teacher is pointing to pictures on the wall of Nansen, wearing furs and standing on the ice with an Inuit man. The display says: 'Nansen learned from the natives and it made him the best explorer in the world.'

Which seems fishy to me cos surely that just means the Inuit were good explorers and Amundsen and Nansen were average Inuit?

The explorers were so racist about the Inuit. It's really gross. Called them 'apes' and 'crossbreeders' and even the word Eskimo is kind of uncool because it meant 'eater of raw meat' and so was kind of an insult which I wouldn't have known if Dad hadn't told me so don't worry if you've always said Eskimo cos not everyone knows. But it was actually really dumb cos the Inuit knew the land better. And all these explorers would make big iron ships to smash the ice and special cans to transport their roast beef and basically try to beat the Arctic through sheer bloody Victorian-ness, and then they'd all get stuck in the ice with scurvy and frostbite and hole up in shitty tents dying miserably and the Inuit would just casually sled up to them in their furs like 'oh hey, how's it going we've just come back from hunting and my wife just gave birth on a sledge NBD.' So a bit rich to then call them savages. But I don't know how to say that in German so I keep quiet.

I follow the school group down the stairs, hoping I can slip away, but some fucking kid turns and sees me and says something in German and then all his friends are looking so I quickly turn off down a corridor, away from them, and into a dark side room. I press against the wall. They don't follow me.

And then I hear this sound –

We hear what RORY *hears.*

It sounds strange. Like water and electricity and static. Creaking old floorboards and whirlwinds. It's ice. Melting, freezing, cracking. The sign says the artist left microphones in glaciers and rocks and collected the recordings and put them together and made this. Weird to think of all those thousands of miles of empty ice, making all this noise with nobody there to listen.

There's a poster on the wall like the ones Mrs Harris makes us
copy of photosynthesis and the nitrogen cycle except this one's
actually pretty cool cos it says the ice is actually like a Swiss
cheese, full of holes, and tiny little things like bacteria and algae
and even baby fishes when they're just born can live in there.
The room is in dark-blue light, and up above us the ceiling
looks like a hard, white cloud. It's like the underneath of an ice
floe. And there's a voice –

VOICEOVER. Light is the pulse of the Arctic. Lys er polen
    i arktisk.

    Sunlight and warm water cause the ice to melt. Sollys og
    varmt vann fører til at isen smelter.

Can you hear, Dad? Doesn't sound real, does it? Sounds kind of
alien. Properly strange. It really does kind of feel like I'm
trapped in ice.

VOICEOVER. In winter the ice grows thicker as the Polar
    Night lengthens. Om vinteren blir isen tykkere som Polar
    Night forlenger.

They found three of Franklin's men buried in the ice and the ice
was so cold their bodies were still perfect like a hundred years
later, they still had eyelashes and everything, like they'd just
gone to sleep instead of dying from lead poisoning.

VOICEOVER. It may look desolate, but the Arctic ice is a
    perfect habitat for many species. Arktisk is er et perfekt sted
    for mange arter.

The ice preserved them perfectly.

RORY *listens to the ice. Eventually the cycles of sound, from
cracking and thawing and melting, slow down and all we are
left with is the sound of the ocean.*

I leave the museum and take Dad to a little square near the
water. I have half a sandwich in my bag. I should really wait
a little longer to eke it out but I'm so hungry I feel a bit shaky.
I eat a pack of sugar too for the energy. There's a statue of
Roald Amundsen right in the middle. Can't bloody move for
explorers in this town. He was the first to get to the South Pole.

He wasn't first to the North Pole, but he did get there in the end, only he went by plane which is sort of cheating. A seagull lands on his head and I realise his eyebrows are covered in shit. (*Holds Dad up*.) Can you see?

It's getting towards evening now and I should probably start looking for somewhere to stay. I'm studying my map when I hear a loud burst of laughter from nearby and I look up and there's a little group of kids maybe my age sitting on the grass laughing and –

There's a boy.

RORY *looks at him and then immediately snaps her head away so as not to be seen looking.*

Oh my god.

Why is there such a difference between boys at school and boys in the wild? He's with two other friends and shit they're cool too. One's got an actual beard but in a way that looks good, not like the ginger bumfluff boys at school are so proud of. And there's a girl with them and I want to pull my hat down over my face completely she's so beautiful and not like TV-beautiful but like, proper-real-beautiful. Like, she's got a fringe and she still looks good that's how pretty she is. I got a fringe once. I looked like an egg in a wig and deleted the photos. Where do women go to learn to be women like that? Bet she's slept with both of them.

And she's laughing. Proper big laugh like I can see her teeth, laughing like it doesn't matter if people look. And both the boys smile and I watch them watch her laughing and my face feels big and my arms feel too long and my legs rub together and my hair is shit, it's not anything you know it's just hair. And I feel stupid because it doesn't matter does it? Nansen didn't sit on his ship worrying about contouring. Maybe Wanny Woldstad did.

They're passing round a bottle and taking sips and beardy man looks up and our eyes lock and oh god he's seen me looking.

RORY *looks away.*

They're talking in Norwegian and I know I just know it's something about the weird little girl staring at them but then –

BEARDY. Hey, excuse me, you want to try?

Beardy says.

RORY. What?

I say.

BEARDY. Aquavit, it's good.

And then Cool Girl speaks to me –

COOL GIRL. We're being so loud, we disturbed you.

And I hear myself stammer –

RORY. Oh no. That's fine.

Like a fucking idiot.

BEARDY. Here. Celebrate with us.

And I don't know what to do and I'm sure my face is burning and then He speaks.

ANDREAS. Ignore him if you want. You don't have to. It's strong stuff.

He says. He's looking at me. And I smile what I hope is a confident but easy-going smile and say

RORY. Yeah alright.

It's a bit weird to be sitting and drinking with a fit boy with your dad's ashes in your backpack.

I decide not to mention it.

His name is Andreas. He's in his last year of school and he's going to university in Oslo next year. Beardy guy is Marius and Cool Girl is, get this, Astrid. Astrid. Even her name is cool. Bitch. And I even quite like her which is weird cos I normally don't get on with girls as much. And none of them know what normal English names are so they all think Rory is normal and I don't have to explain it at all. It's ace.

And I don't think Dad would mind me drinking Aquavit. I'm partaking in a local custom like the explorers who ate whale spine and seal stomachs. And the Aquavit's not bad. If you drink it in small sips.

MARIUS. Hey.

Says Marius.

MARIUS. You could come with us if you want. To the party.
    It'll be fun. Andreas is driving us.

He drives.

I don't have anywhere else to be.

Everyone at the party is impossibly cool. We're all outside and
there's a big bonfire and no adults anywhere, buckets of beers
and music playing. The sun is only just starting to set even
though it's late so everything is red and orange. It's definitely
the coolest party I've ever been too. Like I almost feel cool just
for being here. I drink a beer and feel the cold bubbles in my
mouth and the warm fire on my face. I have this fuzzy feeling,
like nothing's really real and nothing really matters. And I know
I have a mission, and I know this is a detour, but one extra night
can't hurt, right, Dad? Even the explorers had parties on their
ships. And I don't get invited to many parties back home and
when I do they're always rubbish. Bowls of Wotsits and WKDs
in the sink and girls getting fingered on the sofa. And somebody
always gets way too drunk too early and you never want it to be
you. Mum grilling me about it all the next day. Who was there?
What did you do? Et cetera. As if.

Mum will know I'm gone by now.

My backpack feels heavy. My mouth feels thick. Am I drunk?
I don't get drunk often, Dad, promise. The night they told me
you'd died I waited till Mum was asleep and I took a bottle of
something from the cupboard, I was so scared of getting caught
I didn't even look what it was and it was something weird like
Martini mix but I drank all of it. I don't know why. I didn't
really want to. It felt more like acting something someone else
had done. I was still vomiting at three next afternoon, and neat
Martini mix is worse the second time round let me tell you.

Everyone around me is singing. The boy whose birthday it is is
hoisted up onto his friends' shoulders and bounced about.
Everything feels spinny but in a nice way, like I'm right at the

top of the earth and it's all underneath me which I guess it sort of is. And then

Andreas is suddenly beside me

ANDREAS. It's the birthday song.

He says.

RORY. Oh?

ANDREAS. It's what we sing at birthdays. Different to English.

RORY. Yeah.

I say.

ANDREAS. Our song doesn't have the person's name in. It's always the same.

RORY. Oh.

Say something.

RORY. When I was little my dad used to tease me singing 'Happy Birthday' to the wrong name. Like, when it got to 'happy birthday dear…' he'd sing his own name. Or the dog's name, or Mum's name and I'd SCREAM and he'd act all confused.

ANDREAS. He sounds funny.

RORY. Yeah.

I sip my beer. My legs and arms feel all warm and I feel kind of reckless. I can hear myself talking and I actually think I sound good. I sit down in the snow, I've sort of forgotten I have my backpack on so it happens a bit quicker than I'd meant. He says –

ANDREAS. Careful. You English can't drink like we can.

And I hear myself say –

RORY. Wanna bet?

Like a confident girl. He smiles and sits beside me. I trace my fingers in the snow.

RORY. We don't get snow like this in England.

I say. He lights a cigarette. Offers me one. I look at the smoke rising, the paper turning to ash.

RORY. No, thanks.

He shrugs and puts the pack away.

ANDREAS. Here, always snow. Even in the summer. We're
snow people. You cold?

I know this game.

RORY. A little.

He smiles.

ANDREAS. Here.

And he shuffles up even closer beside me.

ANDREAS. Is that alright?

RORY. Goldilocks.

I say.

RORY. Just right.

ANDREAS. Body warmth. Like the Eskimos do. You know
they have many many words for snow?

I don't correct him.

And I don't know what to say so I say –

RORY. There was this explorer called Peter Freuchen and he
spent a whole Arctic winter in a little hut all by himself. And
it was so cold that his breath froze to the walls. And when
they came back to find him he was almost completely
trapped, because the walls were so thick with his frozen
breath. And they had to break him out with chisels.

ANDREAS. Really?

RORY. Yeah, and another time –

And he kisses me.

I've been kissed before. I'm not a total reject. Even dorks
whose dads are teachers rarely make it to fifteen unkissed. But
this is different. Proper. This feels like grown-up kissing, like,
kissing with intent. I want to be kissing him. And for some
reason he wants to be kissing me. And it's lovely cos nobody

here knows who I am. So I could be anyone. I could be the kind of girl who puts her hand on his chest over his coat. Who lets him put his hands inside her jacket. Who puts her tongue in his mouth first. And nobody has to know.

So when he says –

ANDREAS. Do you want to go somewhere?

I think. Fuck it. Yes. I do.

And we get in his car. I put my bag in the boot. And he drives, which is a bit bad cos I know he's been drinking but the roads are totally empty. I've still got some beer and I swig it and my heart pounds and my stomach's all fluttery and my skin feels like snow waiting for footprints. And we get to his and have to be quiet cos his parents are asleep but it's like giggly silly quiet and I can't stop grinning. And I've never done this before but he doesn't ask so I don't tell him.

And he's being so lovely and kissing all over my face and my neck and taking my shirt off I'm just a bit nervous cos nobody's really seen me before, *I* try not to look even and what if he doesn't like it. It's all happening very quickly and I'm in my bra and it's a rubbish one, I mean, I don't really have any nice ones cos there was never much point and is he disappointed? Is he just good at hiding it? I bet he's done this loads and seen loads of girls. He's gonna take my bra off he's going to think my boobs are shit isn't he? Boys at school do this thing where they flick water at your chest and say they're watering your boobs to make them grow. I look at his face to see if it falls. Should I say something so he knows I know they're rubbish? No. Keep smiling, kiss him back, don't just lie there, I don't know much but I now you're just not supposed to just lie there. I've never put a condom on before. It's not like in school with the cucumbers cos it's hard yeah but it's also soft and in school nobody's putting their hands in your pants while you're trying to concentrate, and you can't be too good at it in school or they'll think you're a slag. I haven't shaved I bet he thinks that's gross and I can feel that I'm… wet but am I wet enough like how much is normal, I don't want him to think I'm not enjoying it cos I am and his breathing's gone all funny and he doesn't sound like himself. I put my hand on his… And I sort of squeeze it a bit and I wasn't expecting how the skin sort of *slides* and he makes this kind of grunt and he leans towards me and I lie backwards and I don't like lying on my back cos my boobs go really small and I'm sure he's thinking how small they are and his fingers are... *inside* now and it's a little uncomfortable and it'd be nicer if he moved them a bit slower but I'm sure he knows what he's doing and I'm sure I must have like three chins in this position and then he takes his fingers away and then he. Pushes.

And I knew it was going to hurt like, obviously it hurts but oh shit it hurts.

And I don't want to ruin it.

But like. Does he know how much it hurts?

I hold my breath. And I look at him. He looks totally different. The way he breathes. The way he moves his body. The way he looks at me. Like he's gone somewhere else and I've stayed here.

And afterwards he smiles.

ANDREAS. That was great.

He says. So I guess I did okay.

He brings me a glass of water. I want to brush my teeth but my washbag is in my backpack in the boot of his car with Dad.

He falls asleep. I stare at the ceiling.

I've bled a little. A little red stain on the sheet. He hasn't seen yet which is good cos that's a bit embarrassing, isn't it. I knew that would happen. They warn you in school. About the pain and the bleeding. Like a little period. They tell you a bit what to expect so that was okay.

I guess I'm more surprised by what happened to him than what happened to me

I guess I'd never met the animal in someone before.

Do I have that in me, too?

And I know it sounds silly but I find myself thinking like. Every woman who has ever existed except like nuns I guess but every woman who has ever existed except nuns has been where I am now. Millions of us. Millions of women, and girls, in millions of beds looking at millions of ceilings in every country and every decade in castles and caves and igloos, Inuit women and explorers' wives, acres, miles, continents of bedsheets and millions of little red stains. And I sort of pictured us all lined up in a long chain, one after the other from now till the first woman ever, and I felt like, really felt, like if I craned my head back far enough maybe I could see my mum. And if I looked past my feet I could see my daughter, maybe, I don't know, and tell her. Something.

Some of the explorers shagged Inuit women while on their expeditions. Traded bits of metal for wives. Gave them syphilis. They all wanted to be the first. To stick their flag in the ice. They even call it 'virgin territory', don't they?

I look at Andreas, sleeping. And I can't stay there any more.

I get up. I put back on the clothes I took off before.

I pick his car keys up off the floor. Relax, I'm just getting Dad out the boot. I'm not a thief. Yet. It's 4 a.m. so the sun is up. I put the keys back though the letterbox. I want to say I think about leaving a note but I don't.

I pause when I get round the corner. There's a dull pain between my legs. I open the backpack, brush my teeth and spit into the snow. I take Dad out. I hold him.

RORY *cradles Dad for a moment. She looks at him. But something is different, now. She puts him back.*

Better keep going.

The city looks different today. The fog's rolled in so you can't see across the water. It makes my hair all wet and my face cold. It's too far to walk to the airport so I have to wait for ages at a bus stop all alone and by the time it comes everything's numb. I have to take my glove off to take out coins for the bus and I can't feel my fingers and I don't know what any of them are and I can feel everyone on the bus hating me for being slow. My stomach feels fluttery and my hands are a bit shaky and I guess I haven't eaten anything since yesterday afternoon.

I think I'd let you be run over all over again for a bite of a bacon sandwich right now, Dad.

Joking.

I feel grimy. I haven't showered in a couple of days. My head hurts a little – how many beers did I drink last night? At the airport I go to the toilet and splash my face with soap and cold water, do my pits with a wet wipe. Nice. Look in the mirror.

RORY *looks in the mirror*.

The flights to Svalbard are so much more expensive than I'd thought. Sorry, Mum. Put it on the tab. Everything here is crazy expensive, I do the maths in my head and a cup of coffee and some toast is over a fiver which unless there's like crack in the butter is a total rip-off so I just nab some packs of sugar and tip the granules into my mouth.

On Elisha Kane's expedition they staved off scurvy by eating rats.

At least I'll be super-skinny by the end of this.

There's another woman travelling by herself in the café, drinking a coffee. She's maybe in her sixties, with long grey hair in a plait almost down to her waist which is weird cos usually old ladies cut their hair short don't they? She catches me staring and smiles and sort of nods at me, like, a sharp little nod and I nod back and it feels a bit like a secret handshake. She takes a sip of her coffee and my stomach *howls*.

But it's okay, Dad. Cos soon we will actually be in Svalbard. They've got polar bears there, Dad. Wild ones, not like in a zoo. It's illegal to leave town without a rifle. Imagine. You sort of forget nature's dangerous. Kids bang on the glass of the lions at zoos. But people still get killed by bears, here. Remember how you used to wrap up in a sheet and chase me round the garden like you were a polar bear and I'd run screaming? Maybe now we'll see a real one. Apparently polar bears are eating each other now because the ice is melting so much they can't hunt. Some of them try to swim out to find food and then they drown or they end up on islands where they shouldn't be and then farmers shoot them. Some of them are becoming hermaphrodites cos of the chemicals in the water.

I expect the plane to be like a tiny little biplane or something but it's not, it's proper, and there's families with kids boarding. The first few people who tried to fly over the Pole died or crashed and had to be rescued from ice floes and even Amundsen died in a plane crash or at least, they think he did. His plane went down and his body was never found so who knows. Imagine escaping scurvy and frostbite at both Poles and then dying in a bloody plane crash. And now there's air hostesses in heels and packs of peanuts and recycled air.

I think dying in a plane crash would probably be the worst way to die. You're a little tin tube surrounded by strangers and chances are when you hit the ground you get like, ripped apart or burned up and your body bits get mingled up with the body bits of the strangers near you so even if they do find you and scoop you up it probably won't just be you, but bits of the people next to you too. So the next time you're on a plane take a look at who's next to you cos you may be spending eternity with their jawbone in your coffin.

Turns out I'm sat next to the long-haired old lady. So that'd be alright. I get a better look at her. She's wearing jeans and boots and a thick knitted jumper and it doesn't look like she's wearing any make-up. Her plait is long and messy and she's got deep creases round her eyes but in a nice way. She nods at me again.

LONG-HAIRED OLD LADY. Hei.

RORY. Hey.

She sits with a notebook and – my stomach flips – a pack of crisps. I can smell the salt. I crave it with like, a super-human strength, like with everything in me. She must notice me ogling the packet cos she holds it out

LONG-HAIRED OLD LADY. Vil du ha litt?

RORY. Sorry?

LONG-HAIRED OLD LADY. Would you like some?

RORY. Oh, no thanks.

LONG-HAIRED OLD LADY. You sure? I won't ask again

Beat.

RORY. Okay. Thanks.

I try to be polite and only take a few. The taste of the salt on my lips is one of the loveliest things I've ever experienced. My whole body feels like it surges up and my skin tingles. Fuck science, crisps are definitely good for you. I lean back and look out of the window as we pull away from the gate, from Tromsø, for good maybe. The ocean is ahead and it looks massive, like there can't possibly be any more land out there. Everything is falling away behind me, I can sort of imagine everything getting smaller and smaller like in a car mirror. Home and Mum and even Andreas, getting smaller and smaller till I can blot them out with my thumb and I breathe out my eyes get so heavy and –

I'm on an ice floe.

RORY *is suddenly floating in vast white nothing. She hears water and ice and wind. She is alone, she bobs up and down and the whiteness starts to take shape, dark patches appear, she is on one floe among thousands, floating in a loose mosaic, infinitely far in all directions.*

I look around and as far as I can see is grey sky and thousands of white floes floating on black water. Everything's kind of wobbly, the ice and my body going up and down. Gently. Sea creatures swim the ice. I can't make out what they are. They're deep and dark.

She looks around. Does she hear distant whale song? It is very cold. RORY*'s hands turn to ice. If we could see inside of her, her breath would be freezing in her throat.*

And I am so cold. I look down at my hands and my fingers are turning to brittle icicles. All up my arms my veins go blue and thick with frozen blood and my breath turns so cold the vapour of it's freezing in my throat, freezing my lungs like little twigs in the forest in the snow and soon I'll choke. But I'm not afraid. Because there, across the floe I see the body of a bear, only just dead. An ice bear. A polar bear. A gift I've been given, just for me. I go up to her and I reach out my hand and I touch her fur and it's the softest thing I've ever known and she's going to keep me alive. There's milk leaking from her nipples, thick as cream, and her belly has been cut open. And I know what to do.

I plunge my icicle hands into her hot stomach, and the blood steams up and I stop shivering. And my hands are my own hands again, covered in blood.

(*To the bear.*) Thank you.

RORY *wakes up*.

Was I drooling? Shit, was I drooling? Where are we?

LONG-HAIRED OLD LADY. We're coming in to land.

A voice says. I look blearily at the woman beside me. I hope she didn't see me drooling. I feel funny. My stomach's all fluttery.

RORY. What?

LONG-HAIRED OLD LADY. We're coming in to land.

She says.

I look out the window.

Whoa.

It's just snow and mountains and sky. Mountain right up to the ocean's edge. Everything coated in empty white snow. Men died in their harnesses dragging their sleds across snow like this.

The plane lands.

We're in Svalbard, Dad. Doesn't get much more north than this.

We get off the plane, the lady with the plait passes me, a big khaki backpack flung over her shoulder.

LONG-HAIRED OLD LADY. Have a good trip.

She says.

RORY. You too.

I watch her leave. I go a bit cold as she leaves, which I know is stupid cos I didn't really know her but she's the only grown-up I've spoken more than two words to since I left and now she's gone and I'm starting to realise that the dark side of not having anyone to answer to is also not really having anyone who gives a shit about you. I should've taken more crisps when I had the chance.

Okay. Here goes.

I step outside the airport.

Oh fuck it's cold.

It's cold like an electric shock that doesn't stop.

I left my scarf at the party. I take some leggings out my bag and wrap them round my face.

If I head to town, I can find information.

The wind is properly icy and the ground under me is crunchy and slippy. My heart's a bit fluttery. The mountains are *huge*. And empty. And all around us. Dad, I wish I could hold you but your urn's too cold. The road is quiet, hardly any cars. It becomes very clear very quickly that my boots are not as waterproof as advertised and my socks get soggy with freezing water and my toes are very cold and then they're very numb and I try very hard not to remember how very quickly frostbite happens. If I was doing this trip with Dad he'd've booked a taxi and a hostel and we'd be halfway to town by now and he'd be pointing out interesting geological features. Like –

The mountains here are four hundred million years old and they used to be at the equator, and in four hundred million years they will probably have shifted to the equator again.

And –

Svalbard is sixty per cent glaciers and one hundred per cent permafrost which means the ground never fully warms up even in the summer.

I can't see the airport behind me any more.

The biggest glacier is nearly six hundred metres thick which means even the fastest man in the world would take over a minute to run from the top to the bottom.

Which seems kind of boring in a textbook but absolutely terrifying here.

And I know I shouldn't complain because on Nansen's trip, it got to forty degrees below zero which is definitely worse than this but it really is really quite cold now and then –

There's a car, pulling up beside me. It's slowing down. The back door slides open.

It's the long-haired lady from the plane.

LONG-HAIRED OLD LADY. Need a ride?

She says.

And I know usually hitchhiking is just asking to have your arms cut off by a pervert but I am in that car so fast.

RORY. Thank you.

FRIDA. I'm Frida.

She says.

RORY. Rory.

FRIDA. It's a nasty walk in to town in winter time.

She says.

RORY. Yeah.

FRIDA. What brings you to Svalbard?

I panic a bit.

I say.

RORY. I want to see the bears.

She smiles.

FRIDA. You have to be lucky. Bears are wanderers.

She says.

She's a researcher, from the mainland. She works here sometimes but always comes a bit early so she can paint.

RORY. You're a painter?

She shrugs.

FRIDA. I try.

She's going camping on the peninsula. Getting a boat to the edge of a glacier base and staying there.

RORY. That sounds really nice.

I say.

FRIDA. It is! And what about you?

I sort of shrug. I don't know. I don't know where I'm staying yet.

FRIDA. You're joining a tour?

She asks.

RORY. I don't think so.

She looks me up and down. Probably wondering what kind of idiot I am for not knowing where I'm going.

FRIDA. Would you like to come with me?

She asks.

FRIDA. It's a good place to see the bears.

And I know I should say no but it would be nice to show Dad a bear. And statistically serial killers are usually men.

RORY. You're sure you don't mind?

Her face like lights up with a smile.

FRIDA. Not at all.

She says.

FRIDA. I'd be glad for the company.

I can't believe the strangeness of this place I'm in. I can't believe places like this exist, or that London can still exist right now, at the same time, as this place here. That right now somewhere else people are crammed into the Tube or crossing a busy street or riding a roller-coaster or watching a movie, that all those peopley things are happening somewhere else while this is happening here. We sailed off in a boat from Longyearbyen port and into a *wilderness*. Everything is bright bright blue and white in every shade and I realise I'm probably actually seeing colours I've never even seen before. I always thought whiteness meant no colour, meant like absence, like a blank page, but it isn't. This isn't blank, this isn't absence. I've never seen anything so real in all my life.

Chunks of ice flow and float around us in mad shapes, shapes
made by light and time and water. A huge one drifts past us like
a dinosaur, like a spaceship. I always thought nature made a
kind of sense, like its rules were people-sized. I understand
I think what, like, a dog is or how a tree works. But the shapes
in this iceberg. The grooves and gaps and sluices. It's a
sculpture that a person's never touched, and it's disintegrating
and melting and will disappear and maybe reform again into
new shapes and the laws that make those shapes are ancient and
I don't understand them. Never listened hard enough in
Geography, did I, Dad?

Frida points things out to me as we go. There are actual real-life
reindeer along the shore. I look through her binoculars at birds
with Harry Potter names – red-throated divers, northern
fulmars, ptarmigans and eidars, guillemots and buntings, purple
sandpipers and ivory gulls. And a barnacle goose, cos they can't
all be poetic.

We arrive at the campsite and jump off the boat onto the snowy
shore. The campsite ranger meets us, a big guy with a rifle slung
over his shoulder. He says we can't leave the camp unless we
have a gun with us, there's people standing guard to raise an
alarm if they see a bear.

Frida and I set up her tent, just how Dad and I used to, only hers
is the Real Deal, not an ancient one with broken zips. I have to
take off my gloves to tie the tent strings and my hands go numb
from cold. Frida lights up a little camping stove and makes us
some cups of coffee.

FRIDA. Careful.

She says as she hands it to me. Getting cold is one thing, getting
warm again is when it hurts.

I wince as the feeling comes back into my fingers. The coffee is
strong and sweet and hot, and she's brought biscuits to dunk.
We sit in silence, but like a nice silence, not awkward paws.
Frida unpacks her canvas and starts to paint.

It's evening now, but the sun's not going to set. It sort of just
dips a bit below the horizon. Everything is deep blue, red and

orange, like the clouds are on fire. Behind me is a little row of tents and then a mountain.

(*To Dad*.) You would have loved this.

This is the nicest time to come, Frida says. Everything is melting, changing, the animals returning, the birds laying their eggs. You really see the cycles. The land sheds the ice. The melting happens earlier every year. Places melting completely that never used to melt before.

I watch the sun on the water and the birds flying back to the cliffs. I plant my feet firm on the ground.

I say

RORY. It's weird. When I stand here the whole world is holding me up.

She says

FRIDA. Wherever you stand the whole world is holding you up.

Which I guess is true, isn't it?

Frida's come to work in one of the observation stations. She says you can see stuff in the sky and in space from Svalbard that you can't see from anywhere else in the world, winds from the sun hitting our atmosphere. That's what makes the Northern Lights happen. And it's happening all the time, even when it's bright, just you can only see it when it's dark.

FRIDA. It's a shame you won't see it, though.

She says.

FRIDA. And the stars! When the clouds clear and the stars are out, it's like nothing else.

I say

RORY. You know why it's called The Arctic? Cos the North Star, right above the Pole, is in the constellation called The Great Bear, and the Greek word for bear is arktos. So The Arctic is actually named after a bear. Cool right?

FRIDA. That is very cool.

Frida says.

RORY. And did you know the Pole Star isn't actually one star? It's two stars, orbiting around each other. But you need a really good telescope to see that.

FRIDA. I did know that. Where do you learn all these things?

RORY. From my dad. He loved facts like that.

She smiles.

FRIDA. An interesting man.

RORY. Yeah.

I say.

RORY. He was. He always wanted to come here.

I say.

FRIDA. Really?

RORY. Yeah.

I say. I say

RORY. He died.

She keeps painting.

FRIDA. I'm sorry.

RORY. It's okay.

She says.

FRIDA. I'm sure he's here with you now.

RORY *gives us a smile*.

RORY. I'm sure he is.

FRIDA. And your mother?

RORY. Still alive.

FRIDA. Well. That's good. Grief can be a lonely place. It's good you have each other.

RORY. Yeah.

Frida pauses painting a moment, lowers her brush and looks out at the ocean. I wonder what she sees out there. I look at the canvas. She's painted the mountains on the horizon, the low-hanging sun and the shingly beach and there, on the shore, our little tent, and two tiny figures beside it.

The ranger has a cabin with a little shop. Frida gives me some money to buy us some tins of soup to eat, warns me not to go too far. The rocks of the beach only go a little way before the ice begins. I head towards it, over rocks covered in lichen and moss and flowers Frida called saxifrage and I pause a moment at the line of snow and then place one foot over the edge and step onto it. It crunches under me in thick fragments, shattering into crystals under me and tumbling over the top of my boot. My toes get chilled but it's not so bad knowing I've got a warm tent to go back to. If I look ahead, everything is white, under me and around me and over me. Like when old cartoon characters run off the edge of the drawing. I close my eyes tight and open them again but, nope. Still there. I'm not dreaming.

When we learnt about space at school Mrs Harris showed us a photo taken when they did the moon landing. Everyone knows Neil and Buzz but there was this third guy, Michael Collins, and he stayed in the main ship orbiting the moon waiting for them to finish prancing about in craters and sticking flags in moondust and while he was up there he went right around to the dark side of the moon, the one we don't see, and he took a photo back of the moon and the earth lined up behind it like an eclipse. And he wrote 'Every single human being in the universe is in this photo except for Michael Collins.' I feel like every single human being in the world is far behind me. I can turn my back on all of them if I like.

And I smile. Like, just to myself, not at a joke or anything funny like a smile that bubbles up from inside me even though there's nobody there to smile at so I probably look like a weirdo standing grinning to myself but it feels nice and nobody can see me anyway. Because I think I might make it. And when I get there. When I get there. Well, when I get there, I'll know, won't I, Dad?

I go back to the tent. The fog has really rolled in now and my toes are *freezing*. Imagine being Nansen stuck in the ice in midwinter freezing cold and thinking you might never be warm

again? Frida's finished painting and gone back inside already.
I hope she's made more coffee, I could murder a coffee. I duck
in through the canvas and –

She's holding Dad. And my passport.

RORY. What are you doing?

I say.

FRIDA. Rory.

She says.

FRIDA. Does your mother know you're here?

My heart's thudding. I feel sick. I feel so angry it's like I'm
on fire.

RORY. Those are my things.

FRIDA. Rory, you're too young to be here alone, she'll be
    worried about you. We'll call her in the morning, let her
    know where you are. And this? You can't take this from her.
    These are precious things.

RORY. It's not a thing, it's my dad. Give him back.

I snatch Dad back from her and run from the tent. I almost trip,
stupid fucking ropes, but I straighten up. The fog is thick and
the sky and the sea and the snow all merge together and I run
away from the tents and down to the water's edge but what's the
use? Where can I go?

FRIDA. Rory.

RORY. I'm not calling her.

FRIDA. Rory.

RORY. I'm not.

FRIDA. Come back inside.

A siren wails.

There's a siren or something blaring, a loud whining noise and
a searchlight, but I am not going back inside because what is
there to go back to, just avoiding Mum in the garden and Dad's
empty study and a new geography teacher at school I am *not*

going back without getting you to the North Pole, Dad, I don't care what happens because if you don't make it, if you died and never got there, if you died. Disappointed.

Say something, Dad.

Please.

And Frida's trying to put her arm on my shoulders. I hear footsteps and see the ranger run up, looking angry, rifle in his hands. He says something to Frida in Norwegian, he's shouting.

FRIDA. Rory. Come back inside, now.

Frida says. The ranger stares at me, gun over his shoulder, he's speaking loudly, over the siren, and I don't understand most of it but I hear one word I know. '*Bjorn*' again and again '*bjorn*'. I look over his shoulder towards the edge of camp and for a moment just for a moment I could swear the mist hardens and the white takes shape and I'm sure, I'm almost sure, I see two dark eyes shining.

FRIDA. Rory!

Frida pulls me to my feet. I search the mist again, it's empty white, gone.

FRIDA. Come on.

She leads me in.

She says we'll call the police in the morning. She says she'll take me back to Longyearbyen tomorrow. She says she's sorry.

RORY. I'm taking him to the North Pole.

I say.

Frida looks at me.

FRIDA. Oh Rory.

She says

FRIDA. You can't do that. You're a child.

She smiles. She says

FRIDA. Grief makes us do crazy things. Believe me, I know. But it's time to go home now. Tomorrow.

She says.

Frida takes me to the police station. They let me sit in the office. Bring me a cup of coffee and a blanket. Mostly they leave me alone. They take Dad away which is good cos I can't bring myself to look at him but it feels weird not having him near me. They say my mum's on her way. Frida talks to the police for a bit, in Norwegian. Comes to me. I don't look at her.

FRIDA. I'm sorry that you didn't get to see a bear.

She says.

RORY. You're a shit painter.

I say. She just smiles at me. I hate her. She leaves.

Turns out Mum was looking for me. Called the police. It even made the news. Good clickbait headline I guess. You'll never believe what this teenager did with her dad's ashes.

When the explorer Franklin went missing, his wife kept her faith for years that he'd come back alive. Funded search parties to look for him and his men. Eventually they found a sheet of paper in a cairn in a place called Victory Point, way up on the north coast of King William Island. An official typed document with a handwritten scrawl around the edges 'John Franklin died, June 1847.' There were no survivors. They found a skeleton nearby, bones bleached white from cold and exposure. He had a clothes brush and a pocket comb on him. The comb had hairs still in it. She'd kept looking for five years not knowing he was already dead.

Mum's a widow now, I guess. I hadn't thought of it like that.

Franklin never made it. Nansen never made it, either.

They let me sleep in the station but I don't sleep at all. I stare at the ceiling. I'm lying there next morning and an officer comes in.

POLICE OFFICER. Your mother is here.

He says.

I want the ice to crack beneath me and to sink into the sea.

She comes into the office and sees me. Her eyes are red. She looks so tired. She looks exactly how I feel. There's a moment.

And then she's on me, arms around me, sobbing and squeezing me, just squeezing me, not saying anything just pressing on me tight and rocking. I'm sorry. I say. I'm sorry, I'm sorry, I'm so sorry. And she says nothing just rocks and presses. I feel her tears in my ears.

I tell her everything. The notebook. The beardy men. Tromsø. Andreas. I expect her to get angry at that one but she just sort of closes her eyes, like a long blink, and squeezes my hand. I tell her how sad I am Dad never got to do the thing he wanted to do more than anything, how he never got to be an explorer.

RORY. I miss him, Mum.

MUM. I miss him too. He would have laughed so hard at all of this.

She says.

RORY. He never got here. I say.

She looks at me.

MUM. He got you here, though, didn't he?

She says.

RORY *looks at Mum*.

RORY. Yeah. And you. Are you angry?

MUM. Yes.

She says.

MUM. And impressed.

She looks at me for a moment and then she laughs.

MUM. I had to pick your father up from a police station once, too.

RORY. Shut up

MUM. It's true. He was very drunk and he tried to steal some flowers from a petrol station for me.

RORY. Dad?!

Mum just nods.

RORY. That's amazing. Why didn't I know that?

MUM. It was before you were born. I think he was
    embarrassed.

RORY. What a prat.

They laugh together.

MUM. He always wanted to come here.

She says.

MUM. When we first got married we'd talk about it. Seeing the
    polar bears. The Northern Lights. That's why he named you
    Aurora.

She looks at me.

MUM. God, there's so much of him in you.

She says.

And she gets this funny look and –

MUM. Let's do it.

She says.

MUM. Together.

She says.

RORY. Really?

RORY *grins.*

RORY. Alright.

So it's way too hard to trek to the Pole; we don't really have the
right gear and it takes ages and we're probably not really fit
enough to be honest. But there's a woman who does helicopter
tours. She says conditions aren't great so we can't land on the
ice but we can fly overhead.

MUM. What do you think, Rory?

RORY. Perfect.

It's a beautiful bright clear day in Longyearbyen when we take off from the airfield. Mum looks a bit nervous. She doesn't like flying. I tell her –

RORY. You know the first man who ever flew over the North Pole was called Richard Byrd?

And she laughs cos it's funny but it is also true.

I've never been in a helicopter before but it's ace. It's so loud my heart rattles in my ribs, like I can feel the sound in me. We get these headphones so we can hear the pilot talking through her microphone but we can't hear each other. Mum's holding Dad on her lap, like clutching him. I wonder what she's thinking. She stares down at him all through take-off and I really want to talk to her, to tell her I know it's scary but she should look out the window cos she won't want to miss it, but she'd never hear me so instead I lean forward and touch her knee gently and point.

She looks out and her mouth opens.

Cos it's pretty amazing.

Nothing. Amazing nothing. Nothing people died finding. Nothing full of bleached bones and tiny creatures and singing ice. I look at her looking at it and I'm glad she's seen it. I'm glad I'm not going to be the only one of us who's seen it. Like, for both of us now, wherever we are we'll always have been here.

Underneath us the patches of ocean get smaller and smaller until it's nothing at all but ice. We're getting closer and closer to the very top of everything, to where my shitty little compass in the woods used to point to, to north. Dad always said if you can find north, you can find your way home.

It gets windier the further we go and it's proper loud, the blades and the wind roaring in my ears.

PILOT. We're almost there. Up ahead.

The pilot crackles in my ears.

Mum and I lock eyes. We didn't talk about this bit, before. What we were going to do. I never thought about it, either. I didn't know what I would do when it came to it. But now it seems clearer than anything, and I know what she's going to do before she does it.

Because it's a shame to come all this way and not make the last few feet.

And he would've hated that urn.

PILOT. Okay. There she is.

I look out. Up ahead, there's a red-and-white striped pole stuck into the ice. It's so unremarkable, one patch of ice among thousands. But it's there. This is it, Dad. We made it. But you have to do the last bit on your own.

Mum shunts down the little perspex window. The wind is ferocious. Mum takes off a glove.

She pauses a moment. Looks at the urn. At Dad. I can see her hands are shaking. I reach out and hold the urn steady so she can unscrew the lid. We each take Dad in our hands.

The rotors of the helicopter and the wind are almost deafening. All around us is the snow. The blizzard, flakes of it swirling like sparrows. She takes a breath, we hold gloves and we let him go.

And all he has to do now is the last few feet to the ground. But the wind is too strong, it's blowing in all directions and the propellers aren't helping and it'd be funny if it weren't so awful but as we scatter the ashes out, they get caught in the wind and blown upwards, up and away from the ice, and at first I want to scream I want to scream at him THAT WAY, Dad, you're SO CLOSE, so close, Dad, please THAT WAY, GO DOWN what are you DOING but then I remember and my heart hurts and my mouth smiles and something like a gasp or a sob or something pushes its way up and out –

Because there's not just one North Pole is there. There's five –

Geographic. Magnetic. Geomagnetic. Inaccessible.

And Celestial.

When you get to the end of something and you look back at the
beginning, you realise all the different ways it could have gone.
If I hadn't left exactly when I did. If I hadn't gone to the polar
museum or met Andreas or Frida. If I'd told Mum right at the
start. If I'd walked home with Dad that day. If Mum and Dad
had never met, never been in love, never made me… If Fridjof
Nansen had been a taxi driver instead of an explorer. The way
things are starts to seem pretty fragile when you think of it
like that.

I'd like to have been nicer to Frida.

We came home soon after the helicopter. It was quicker on the
way back. Mum had to get back to work, and school's starting.
I've decided to start back after the holidays. Mum turns the key
in the door. Steps inside the living room. Nothing's changed and
everything's changed. Wherever we are, we know the ice is still
out there, I guess.

Mum squeezes my shoulder.

RORY. You alright?

I ask.

MUM. Goldilocks.

She says.

I go into Dad's study. The study. I want to return the book, the
notebook, put everything back in its place, you know. I catch
sight of something on the floor. An old photograph. It must have
fallen out of the notebook when I picked it up.

It's of me and Mum. Dad must have taken it. It looks like our
garden, but I almost don't recognise it at first cos it's covered in
snow. I'm maybe seven or eight in a puffy pink ski-suit, Mum's
in a furry headband. We're chucking balls of snow around,
Mum's got this big grin, her nose and cheeks are red from the
cold and she's just let a snowball fly and it's caught by the
camera in mid-flight, about to hit me, and I'm running towards
the camera and we're both smiling so much you can see our
teeth. In the background there's a snowman we must've built
together. Me and Mum.

I turn the photo over to see if he's written the date on it and.
He's written a quote out from Nansen on the back.

It says –

'Love is life's snow. It falls deepest and softest into the gashes
left by the fight – whiter and purer than snow itself.'

Mum's calling me from the kitchen, asking if I want a cup of
tea, and if we should order takeaway for dinner.

We'll have to clear this room out some time. No sense keeping
all this stuff, really. Put new posters up, plan a new trip.
Somewhere warm. I leave the notebook, I leave Nansen, I leave
the maps and the dead beardy explorers. I take the photo and
I go to the kitchen. I'm going to tell Mum I'd love a cup of tea,
and that a pizza sounds great. I'm gonna show her the photo of
us together in the snow. I think it'll make her smile.

The End.

DISTANT EARLY WARNING

Distant Early Warning was first performed at The Miniaturists, Arcola Theatre, London, on 10 September 2017, with the following cast:

CLARY	Serena Flynn
MARET	Melissa Parker
FRANK	Andrew McDonald
Director	Lucy Jane Atkinson

Characters

FRANK, *male, fifties, English, northern*
MARET, *female, ten. Mimics Frank's accent*
CLARY, *female, twenties, English, southern*

We are in a hut on what once was Greenland in the year 2053.
On a table in the corner is a radio and sonar equipment.
FRANK *is telling* MARET *a story. His clothes look standard-*
issue, a nondescript uniform. Hers are more cobbled together.
His rifle is leant up against his chair, within arm's reach.

FRANK. So he's driving, right, fast as he can, but then this
    helicopter starts circling and chasing him and he can't
    shake it –

MARET. The helicopter's the one like a bird?

FRANK. Right. So he's driving and he's driving and the
    helicopter's circling and he gets to the end of the road, up
    ahead, like a pier –

MARET. A pier?

FRANK. Like a bit of road that goes out over the water –

MARET. Like a *bridge*?

FRANK. Yeah like half a bridge –

    MARET *mouths 'half a bridge' to herself.*

    – and the water's getting closer and closer and the helicopter
    is overhead like *chka-chka-chka-chka* –

    MARET *laughs.*

    – and Amasova's screaming 'WATCH OUT JAMES!' but he
    drives *whoooosh* right off the edge and *splash* lands into the
    water and they're sinking, sinking, sinking and it's all over
    and done and for anyone else this would be the end but a bit
    of ocean never stopped James Bond, this is the British Secret
    Service we're talking about, so up comes a special secret spy
    button on the car controls and – (*Mimes pressing a big*
    button.) BAM – the car turns into a submarine!

MARET. Whoaaa.

FRANK. The wheels disappear and propellers come out and, and he gets this little sonar display –

MARET. Like yours!

FRANK. Just like mine and the helicopter's still overhead but not for long. (*Bond voice*.) 'It's time we got rid of these uninvited guests' and – (*Missile noise*.) he fires a missile, right at it, using the sonar and BLAM it hits it and explodes into a million pieces and he looks at Amasova and he says – (*Bond voice*.) 'Alone at last.' Good, right?

MARET (*a little unsure*). Yeah. Was there somebody inside the hekelopter?

FRANK. Helicopter. Probably. Some Russian. The baddies, Maret. So, –

MARET. Did you go in a hekelopter?

FRANK. Helicopter. Once. On holiday. At the Grand Canyon.

MARET. What's that?

FRANK. It was this big crack in the ground. Really old. You could see all the layers. Kind of overrated.

MARET. Back in England?

FRANK. America.

MARET. You went to *America*?

FRANK (*a little stern*). Don't you want the rest of the story?

MARET. Yes.

FRANK. Right. So. James and Amasova –

The sonar starts to bleep. FRANK *and* MARET *look at it.* FRANK *goes over to the console and taps at the keyboard, is about to push a final button.*

MARET. Can I do it?

FRANK *shrugs. She rushes over. Presses a button. They wait. The bleeping stops.* MARET *beams up at* FRANK.

FRANK. Good job.

Suddenly the door bursts open and CLARY *storms in. She's in
fatigues, trousers, T-shirt and vest, scarf around her lower
face holding up a gun.* MARET *screams.* FRANK *pulls her
away.* CLARY *sees* MARET *and seems to hesitate allowing*
FRANK *to grab his gun. The following happens very quickly.*

Get back.

CLARY. Officer Carter?

FRANK. Who the fuck are you?

CLARY. Drop your weapon.

FRANK. Do I look like a fucking amateur? I'm not taking
orders from you.

CLARY. MOD sent me. Drop the weapon and ID yourself.

FRANK. You're the one stumbling into a classified base with
your gun out. You're a Scandi scout for all I know.

CLARY. And for all I know you're a Russian infiltrator, we've
all got to be cautious, officer.

MARET *takes a little step forward, fascinated by* CLARY.
FRANK *puts an arm out to stop her, lowers his gun for a
moment.* CLARY *takes another step in.*

FRANK. Whoa there. Easy. Alright.

*He very slowly lowers his gun, never taking his eyes off her.
She does the same, at the same slow speed. They roll their
sleeves up to reveal QR tattoos, which they each scan,
cautiously.*

Alice Clary. You sound southern.

CLARY. I got out.

FRANK. Lucky you.

CLARY. Some operatives in the Arctic DEW bases have been
compromised. MOD are doubling up officers. Self-policing,
I guess.

FRANK. I haven't heard anything about that.

CLARY. They're hardly going to give it fanfare, are they?

FRANK. I haven't been 'compromised'.

CLARY. Then you have nothing to worry about. (*To* MARET, *awkward child-friendly voice*.) And who are you?

FRANK. My mascot. Aren't you, Maret? She's with me.

MARET. Are you from England?

CLARY. Yes.

MARET. Do you know James Bond, too?

CLARY. Um?

FRANK. Maret go get a bed roll from the store room. There's a girl.

MARET *looks at him, not wanting to leave, but obeys*.

CLARY (*gesturing after her*). How –

FRANK. My predecessor didn't think much of the government guidelines on native socialisation.

CLARY. She's a native?

FRANK. Half a native. When the ice melted her family went further north with the rest of the indigenous. Left her here. Abandoned her. I haven't told HQ, I don't / want –

CLARY. I won't tell them.

Beat. FRANK *sizes up* CLARY.

Look. I know you have a… system in place here. I don't want to disrupt. I'm here to help.

FRANK. Any news? They tell us nothing.

CLARY. Manhattan went dark. I heard there was / a distress call from –

FRANK. No I mean, is the border holding?

CLARY. Which one?

He gives her a look as if it should be obvious.

They all are. For now.

FRANK. Fucking parasites.

CLARY. Yeah.

MARET *calls from off.*

MARET. I can't see them.

FRANK (*to* MARET). I'll come out. (*Back to* CLARY. *Grudging.*) Well. It's nice to hear another English voice. Even a southern one.

He goes. CLARY *stands for a moment, makes sure he's not coming back. Lets out a breath, as though every muscle has been tensed.*

CLARY (*under her breath*). Fuck.

She hurries to the computer and radio. Finds a frequency.

Can you hear me? Jonah this is Clary, can you hear me? Delay the consignment, okay? Delay the consignment. There's a complication, I couldn't. There's a child here. Just. I'm undercover now. Wait until morning. Delay the consignment, okay?

MARET. That's not a toy.

CLARY *drops the receiver. Recovers.*

CLARY. I know.

MARET. Frank uses that to hunt the monsters.

CLARY. Does he?

MARET. Yeah. The machine finds the monsters, it goes boopboopboop and Frank presses a button and it stops the monsters coming. Who were you talking to?

CLARY. My commander. Just letting them know I got here safely.

MARET. Is it dangerous to come here?

CLARY. It's not safe.

MARET. From England.

CLARY. That's right. Same as Frank.

MARET. You don't sound like him.

CLARY. I'm from a different part of England.

MARET. Which part?

CLARY. It was called Kent. I haven't… It's not there any more.

MARET. Where did it go?

Beat. CLARY *doesn't know what to say.*

England sounds great.

CLARY. Yes. Maybe you'll go there one day.

MARET. I don't have to go there. Frank says England's coming here.

Scene Two

The same. Later. MARET *and* CLARY.

MARET. Have you seen a car?

CLARY. Yes.

MARET. Have you seen a submarine?

CLARY. Yes.

MARET. Have you seen a *pier*?

CLARY. No.

MARET. Have you seen a unicorn?

CLARY. I don't think they exist.

MARET. Yeah. Frank said. They have one horn in the middle and their skin is all grey and scaly.

CLARY. That's a rhinocerous.

MARET. Have you seen one?

CLARY. Yes.

MARET. They have them in England?

CLARY. No. Well. Yeah but in zoos.

MARET. What's zoos?

CLARY. It's where we put the animals so we could see them.

MARET. All the animals?

CLARY. Lots of them.

MARET. England sounds amazing.

CLARY. It's alright.

MARET. It sounds *amazing*. I can't wait.

CLARY. What's Frank told you, then? About England?

MARET. That it's really green but it has white cliffs and castles and forests and lakes and there used to be dragons before King George killed them, and there's big mountains and valleys and trains that go really fast and big bridges to drive over in lorries and Feats of Engineering and there's free hoppitals and all the medicine in the whole world is totally free and there's strawberries growing everywhere and apples too just like falling from the trees into your hands and something called rhubarb? And everyone there is a scientist or a spy or a king or a soldier or a really good runner, and everyone has a Good Sense of Humour and everyone's brave. And the places have cool names like Humber and Whitby and Skye.

CLARY. That's Scotland.

MARET. Yeah and Scotland. He never said about Kent though.

CLARY. No. I shouldn't think he would.

MARET. What happened to it?

CLARY. It flooded.

   MARET *looks blank*.

   It's underwater.

MARET. Why?

   Beat. CLARY *thinks*.

CLARY. Well. You know how everything here used to be covered in snow?

MARET (*uncertain*). Yeah…

CLARY. It did. And all the sea was covered in ice. It used to be freezing up here, everyone wore furs to keep warm it was so cold. But then the ice and the snow melted, and it turned into water, and the water went into the ocean, but there wasn't enough room in the ocean for all the water so the oceans got fuller and fuller and all these places that had been by the sea, or by rivers, or below the level of the sea, were flooded.

MARET. Flooded.

CLARY. Exactly.

MARET. So. Kent is underwater.

CLARY. Kent is underwater.

MARET. Have you seen it underwater?

CLARY. We sailed over the top of my family's house on a boat.

MARET. What happened to the people?

CLARY. Some made it to the north before the border shut. Some stayed. There's some islands left. Oxford. Coventry. Some drowned. (*Suddenly more urgent.*) Maret. Where are your family?

MARET. Frank's my family.

CLARY. No, your real family, your mum, where are they?

MARET. I don't know. Frank said they went away. They didn't like the heat.

CLARY. So you have nowhere to go?

MARET. Why would I go somewhere?

FRANK *enters with bowls of food.*

FRANK. Spag bol, thankyouverymuch. The rations aren't bad you know. Vac-packed bits of home. Can probably dig out a tin of custard. And look at this – English wine. Can you believe it? Yorkshire vineyards. Every cloud, eh?

CLARY. Oh, thanks / but –

MARET. Have you been to America?

CLARY. No.

FRANK. Maret.

MARET. What?

FRANK. They're the baddies, stop this obsession.

MARET. I thought that was Russians.

CLARY. I've never been.

FRANK. It's not safe there, Maret. It's lawless. Bands of Yank
thugs and thieves. Desert towns. America's over. (*To*
MARET, *about her food.*) It's hot, love, blow on it first.

He blows on MARET*'s fork for her. She feeds him
a mouthful.*

CLARY. They've annexed Baffin Island, now.

FRANK. Too close for fucking comfort.

CLARY. They've got to go somewhere.

FRANK. There's barely enough room for us Brits, love, let
alone a billion displaced Yanks. (*Laughs.*) You wanna share
your bunk with some half-starved redneck you be my guest
but you can do it in your own bloody cabin. Can't feed a
nation on bleeding hearts. Maret stop picking out the carrots.

MARET. I'm not.

FRANK. Well what's that then? Come on, they're good for you.
Help you see in the dark.

MARET *rolls her eyes.*

No roast dinner but it's not bad.

CLARY. It's nice. Thank you.

FRANK. You can thank me by taking the night shift. I can get
some proper bloody kip for once.

CLARY. Tonight?

FRANK. Oh got other plans, have you?

CLARY. No.

FRANK. Well then. (*Beat. He eyes her up.*) You've not done it before.

CLARY. I have.

MARET. It's easy, Clary. I can show you.

CLARY. No, / I have –

FRANK (*to* MARET). Sit down. Only girls who've eaten all their carrots can operate the radar.

MARET. Frank –

FRANK. I don't make the rules.

MARET. You so do though –

CLARY. I know how it works. I've been trained. I'm happy to take the shift tonight. Do you get much – (*Searches for the word.*) action –

FRANK. Two or three a day. And rising. More all the time.

CLARY. Mainly Scandinavian, or?

FRANK (*shrugs*). They all look the same on the bleeper.

Scene Three

Later that night. CLARY *is awake. She speaks into the radio in a whisper.*

CLARY. Jonah? I don't know if you can hear me. But I'm disabling now. Good luck. I'll see you all on the other side. (*Beat.*) I love you.

The lights flick on. FRANK *is there, holding his gun, not pointed at her yet.*

FRANK. Who were you talking to, Alice Clary?

CLARY. HQ. Just updating / them –

FRANK. I looked you up. Alice Clary. Turns out Alice Clary was on riot control. Down at the border. 'Cept she went Missing in Action six months ago and hasn't been found. My guess is when they find her she'll be missing a tattoo. Who were you talking to?

Beat. CLARY *lunges for her gun,* FRANK *points his at her.*

I wouldn't.

CLARY. We're called the Southern Refugee Alliance.

FRANK. Southern Refugees.

CLARY. The south was hit hard, whole cities underwater, we need to help / people –

FRANK. Alright, girl, that's enough. I don't want to hurt you. I want you to stop this silliness. Step away from my machines. Go out that door. Go back wherever took you in. Thank your stars you got out when you did, that we gave you shelter when shelter was scarce.

CLARY. And what about the others? There are thousands of survivors, we're trying to get them out but you keep shooting them out of the water, these are English people.

FRANK. I've seen them on the news, these English people. Rioting and looting and fighting over aid boxes, ripping rations from each other's mouths, children abandoned. That's not my England.

CLARY. They're desperate.

FRANK. What's that to me? It's maths, girl. Dividing what we got amongst those that need it. We got to look out for ourselves.

CLARY. Who's ourselves? Who's we? How small can you make that word?

MARET runs in.

MARET. Frank?

FRANK. Maret –

CLARY grabs MARET and pulls her, struggling, using her as a human shield.

MARET. Frank! Stop, let go –

CLARY. You want to come to England, Maret? I can take you to England, what's left of England, I can take you tonight, but you have to help me first, okay?

The sonar starts beeping, getting gradually faster through the following.

MARET. Frank! Help!

CLARY is putting pressure on MARET's throat.

CLARY. I don't want to do this.

FRANK. Let her go.

CLARY. There are children on these boats, Frank. Just like her.

MARET. Frank.

FRANK. You let her go.

CLARY. They have to go somewhere. They're your people, Frank.

FRANK fires two shots. CLARY drops. She's dead. MARET is hurt, badly. FRANK rushes to her, cradles her. She is dying.

MARET. Frank.

FRANK. It's alright. It's alright. You're alright.

MARET. I feel cold.

FRANK. It's alright.

MARET. Frank. The monsters.

> FRANK *goes to the sonar. Types. Presses the button. He returns to* MARET.

Was. Was Clary a baddie?

FRANK. Yes. She was a baddie.

MARET. Am I a baddie, Frank?

FRANK. No, no of course not. You're a hero.

MARET. Like James Bond.

FRANK. Like James Bond. Heroes make sacrifices.

> *The beeping stops.*

MARET. Alone at last.

Other Titles in this Series

Annie Baker
THE FLICK
JOHN

Mike Bartlett
ALBION
BULL
GAME
AN INTERVENTION
KING CHARLES III
SNOWFLAKE
WILD

Chris Bush
THE ASSASSINATION OF
    KATIE HOPKINS
STEEL

Jez Butterworth
THE FERRYMAN
JERUSALEM
JEZ BUTTERWORTH PLAYS: ONE
MOJO
THE NIGHT HERON
PARLOUR SONG
THE RIVER
THE WINTERLING

Caryl Churchill
BLUE HEART
CHURCHILL PLAYS: THREE
CHURCHILL PLAYS: FOUR
CHURCHILL PLAYS: FIVE
CHURCHILL: SHORTS
CLOUD NINE
DING DONG THE WICKED
A DREAM PLAY *after* Strindberg
DRUNK ENOUGH TO SAY
    I LOVE YOU?
ESCAPED ALONE
FAR AWAY
HERE WE GO
HOTEL
ICECREAM
LIGHT SHINING IN
    BUCKINGHAMSHIRE
LOVE AND INFORMATION
MAD FOREST
A NUMBER
PIGS AND DOGS
SEVEN JEWISH CHILDREN
THE SKRIKER
THIS IS A CHAIR
THYESTES *after* Seneca
TRAPS

debbie tucker green
BORN BAD
DEBBIE TUCKER GREEN PLAYS: ONE
DIRTY BUTTERFLY
EAR FOR EYE
HANG
NUT
A PROFOUNDLY AFFECTIONATE,
PASSIONATE DEVOTION TO
    SOMEONE (– *NOUN*)
RANDOM
STONING MARY
TRADE & GENERATIONS
TRUTH AND RECONCILIATION

Sam Holcroft
COCKROACH
DANCING BEARS
EDGAR & ANNABEL
PINK
RULES FOR LIVING
THE WARDROBE
WHILE YOU LIE

Vicky Jones
THE ONE
TOUCH

Anna Jordan
CHICKEN SHOP
FREAK
POP MUSIC
THE UNRETURNING
YEN

Lucy Kirkwood
BEAUTY AND THE BEAST
    with Katie Mitchell
BLOODY WIMMIN
THE CHILDREN
CHIMERICA
HEDDA *after* Ibsen
IT FELT EMPTY WHEN THE
    HEART WENT AT FIRST BUT
    IT IS ALRIGHT NOW
LUCY KIRKWOOD PLAYS: ONE
NSFW
TINDERBOX

Rose Lewenstein
COUGAR
DARKNET
FUCKING FEMINISTS
NOW THIS IS NOT THE END

Clare McIntyre
LOW LEVEL PANIC
MY HEART'S A SUITCASE
    & LOW LEVEL PANIC
THE MATHS TUTOR
THE THICKNESS OF SKIN

Sam Potter
HANNA

Jack Thorne
2ND MAY 1997
BUNNY
BURYING YOUR BROTHER IN
    THE PAVEMENT
A CHRISTMAS CAROL *after* Dickens
HOPE
JACK THORNE PLAYS: ONE
JUNKYARD
LET THE RIGHT ONE IN
    after John Ajvide Lindqvist
MYDIDAE
THE SOLID LIFE OF SUGAR WATER
STACY & FANNY AND FAGGOT
WHEN YOU CURE ME
WOYZECK *after* Büchner

Phoebe Waller-Bridge
FLEABAG

Joe White
MAYFLY

A Nick Hern Book

This single edition of *A Hundred Words for Snow* first published in Great Britain in 2019 as a paperback original by Nick Hern Books Limited, The Glasshouse, 49a Goldhawk Road, London W12 8QP

First published by Nick Hern Books in *Heretic Voices* in 2018

A Hundred Words for Snow copyright © 2018 Tatty Hennessy
Distant Early Warning copyright © 2019 Tatty Hennessy
Introduction copyright © 2019 Tatty Hennessy

Tatty Hennessy has asserted her moral right to be identified as the author of these works

Cover image by Madison Clare

Designed and typeset by Nick Hern Books, London
Printed in Great Britain by Mimeo Ltd, Huntingdon, Cambridgeshire PE29 6XX

A CIP catalogue record for this book is available from the British Library

ISBN   978 1 84842 825 6

CAUTION   All rights whatsoever in these plays are strictly reserved. Requests to reproduce the text in whole or in part should be addressed to the publisher.

Amateur Performing Rights   Applications for performance, including readings and excerpts, by amateurs in the English language throughout the world should be addressed to the Performing Rights Manager, Nick Hern Books, The Glasshouse, 49a Goldhawk Road, London W12 8QP, *tel* +44 (0)20 8749 4953, *email* rights@nickhernbooks.co.uk, except as follows:

New Zealand: Play Bureau, PO Box 9013, St Clair, Dunedin 9047, *tel* (3) 455 9959, *email* info@playbureau.com

United States and Canada: Berlin Associates, as below

Professional Performing Rights   Applications for performance by professionals in any medium and in any language throughout the world should be addressed to Berlin Associates, 7 Tyers Gate, London SE1 3HX, *fax* +44 (0)20 7632 5296, *email* agents@berlinassociates.com

No performance of any kind may be given unless a licence has been obtained. Applications should be made before rehearsals begin. Publication of these plays does not necessarily indicate their availability for amateur performance.

Woodland
CARBON
www.woodlandcarbon.co.uk
NICK HERN BOOKS
Printed on Carbon Captured paper

www.nickhernbooks.co.uk

facebook.com/nickhernbooks

twitter.com/nickhernbooks